THE CAVALRY

IN THE

RUSSO-JAPANESE WAR

LESSONS AND CRITICAL CONSIDERATIONS

COUNT GUSTAV WRANGEL

(AUSTRIAN CAVALRY)

TRANSLATED FROM THE GERMAN BY

J. MONTGOMERY

LIEUTENANT 3RD HUSSARS

The Naval & Military Press Ltd

❖

Reproduced by kind permission of the Central Library,
Royal Military Academy, Sandhurst

Published by

The Naval & Military Press Ltd

Unit 10, Ridgewood Industrial Park,

Uckfield, East Sussex,

TN22 5QE England

Tel: +44 (0) 1825 749494

Fax: +44 (0) 1825 765701

www.naval–military-press.com

www.military-genealogy.com

© The Naval & Military Press Ltd 2010

The Naval & Military Press ...

...offer specialist books for the serious student of conflict. The range of titles stocked covers the whole spectrum of military history with titles on uniforms, battles, official histories, specialist works containing Medal Rolls and Casualties Lists, and numismatic titles for medal collectors and researchers.

The innovative approach they have to military bookselling and their commitment to publishing have made them Britain's leading independent military bookseller.

TRANSLATOR'S PREFACE

THE translation of this work was undertaken in the hope that it might be of some use to those British officers who feel interested in the work of the cavalry arm in the Russo-Japanese War. The scope and purpose of the work appear in the author's introduction.

Thanks are due to Herr Von Donat for his kind assistance in revising the proofs.

J. M.

CONTENTS

THE CAVALRY
IN THE RUSSO-JAPANESE WAR

LESSONS AND
CRITICAL CONSIDERATIONS

I

INTRODUCTION

IT appears almost as if the poor performance of the cavalry in the Russo-Japanese War has exercised a paralysing effect on the pens of those who are qualified to criticize it.

Though the literature of the late campaign, in a general way, already shows quite a considerable library, in its purely cavalry branch it is still very badly provided for. This is a decided neglect which, according to our idea, in the interests of the future of cavalry, should be redressed as soon as possible.

The common talk about the complete inaction of the cavalry arm during the Manchurian campaign has brought to light a series of erroneous impressions, which have recently been revived.

It is the intention of this work to combat these decisively, before they are disseminated further.

Our conviction that a strong cavalry, now as formerly, forms an absolutely necessary fighting force for every modern army is supported by a powerful ally. According to the latest reports, it is the intention of the leaders of the Japanese army to form not less than eight divisions of cavalry in the course of the impending reorganization of the army. This means a doubling of the cavalry force which was hitherto available.

Now, the Japanese have without doubt proved that they are an eminently practical people. They are certainly proof against the reproach that out of a love of obsolete tradition they wish to maintain expensive and useless troops for show purposes. If they increase their cavalry, there is no doubt that they do so with the full recognition that the small numbers of this arm prevented them from reaping the full measure of their successes in the late war.

It is not only in order to at once be able to contend with the arguments against a diminution or transformation of the cavalry that the specialist should study the cavalry operations of the late campaign.

Sins of omission, with their drastic results, frequently offer more convincing lessons than the most successful feat of arms.

Even if the debatable points in the tactics of

cavalry have received no clear answer through the experiences of the war in the Far East, yet this arm can partly apply to itself the new clues which were obtained there as far as concerns the two other principal arms.

The employment of cavalry, in battle especially, must be managed in quite another way, in face of the much greater extent of fighting front, the long duration of battles, and the artificial strengthening of positions.

As no large cavalry actions were really fought, there can be no decision as to the relative advantages of line *versus* group tactics, of sword *versus* lance.

On the other hand, in the execution of a few very interesting raids, one is able to recognize the fundamental principles in the carrying out of which success may be achieved. As far as the reconnoitring of both combatants is concerned, so far only can the outline of the whole picture be determined. Before the parties themselves concerned have spoken, and the respective general staff works have thrown more light over the many details of which the duty of reconnaissance is compounded, no final judgment can be passed.

In due time this final judgment is sure to modify in several instances the hypothesis, established by too hasty critics, that the cavalry on both sides was a complete failure.

We will limit ourselves in this work to the

discussion of the following questions (leaving out, for the present, discussion of details which are as yet not sufficiently established) :

1. What has been done ?

2. What ought to have been done ?

3. To what causes are the sins of omission to be attributed ?

4. Is sufficient care taken that our cavalry, if put to the test, could carry out their duties better ?

Only by giving a completely impartial reply to the last point are we able to turn to proper account the experiences of the campaign, and be of some real use to the cavalry arm.

II

THE PERFORMANCES OF THE CAVALRY IN THE RUSSO-JAPANESE WAR

(a) THE RUSSIANS.

THE immense respect with which the whole of Europe regarded the empire of the Czar before the war with Japan, arose in the first instance from the high esteem in which its military power was held.

There was really little justification, from all we had previously heard and seen of it, for the esteem in which the Russian army was held. Numbers were too much thought of, otherwise it would have been scarcely possible to forget that the Russian army, in spite of her almost inexhaustible resources, neither specially excelled in the Crimea nor in the Turkish campaign of 1877-1878.

In the former she was unable to save Sebastopol; in the latter, if it had not been for the timely help of the Roumanians, she would have been defeated at Plevna.

The first-rate qualities of her soldiers—obstinate bravery, blind obedience and attachment, physical endurance—were severely handicapped by the defects in leadership and administration, and by the passive character of her people.

Indeed, it cannot be denied that in Russia the years of peace from 1878-1904 have been used to get rid of, as far as possible, the shortcomings in all branches of the army which came to light during the Turkish campaign. For example, the administration, in the Manchurian theatre of war, worked without a hitch.

Nevertheless, all the improvements and reforms were not able to raise the spirit and morale of the army sufficiently high to engage success-fully in a war against such an opponent as Japan.

The causes why the moral qualities of the Russian army leave much to be desired are rooted deep in the whole system. It would carry us too far if we were to lay them all bare here. For our purpose it is sufficient to state that a lax discipline, aversion to responsibility, rivalry, and inordinate longing after pleasure in the higher ranks, want of enthusiasm and martial ardour in the army generally, led much more to defeat than the mistakes of the much-censured Com-mander-in-Chief.

The critics of the campaign have frequently forgotten to take into consideration, in favour of the much-abused General Kuropatkin, a psycho-logical fact which doubtless weighed upon him heavily. This accomplished soldier already knew the Japanese soldier before the outbreak of the war. The enormous difference in morale between the two armies was no secret to him from the very beginning.

The first encounters, specially the storming of the heights of Kintschou, must have strengthened him in this knowledge. From the feeling of inferior quality of his own forces must have sprung to a great extent the want of initiative and hesitating leadership with which he has been so much reproached.

Also, in criticizing the power of initiative of the Russian cavalry Generals, we must not forget to consider the above-mentioned psychological fact.

The quintessence of all admiration and esteem, bestowed upon the army of the Czar by the public opinion of Europe before the commencement of the campaign, was without doubt apportioned to the Russian cavalry.

When, about twenty years ago, the political sky became overcast, Germany and Austria beheld in spirit their frontier provinces already overrun with numberless hostile mounted hosts. Even the leading military authorities suffered under this delusion. When the clouds which covered the sky of peace had cleared, there still remained respect for the great superiority of the numbers of the Russian cavalry, their warlike training, their dismounted attack, their excellent material, and their immense endurance.

Some few specialists, however, possessed a deeper insight even then.

They did not allow themselves to be deceived as to the true state of affairs by the numbers on paper, the bayonet attack of dismounted cavalry regiments, the distance marches by ice and snow, and the different equestrian tricks of the Cossacks.

The small value of the Cossack organizations for a modern war, the insufficient intelligence of the officers and men of the cavalry of the line, and the one-sided training of the whole of the cavalry, was no secret to them. Yet even these exact judges of the situation did not doubt that the Japanese cavalry, weak, and by repute of inferior quality, must be beaten out of the field. Afterwards it would not be difficult for the Russian cavalry divisions to prepare the greatest diffi-culties in the Manchurian plains for the advance of the opposing hosts.

Though, as a matter of fact, it turned out quite differently, nevertheless we must not be misguided in condemning the whole of the Russian cavalry off-hand.

The contingent that was told off to the Man-churian field army (at Mukden Kuropatkin had at his disposal over 149 squadrons and sotnias) appears more than ample for the execution of the duties apportioned to cavalry. However, as far as their quality was concerned, scarcely two-thirds of them can be looked upon as efficient mounted troops. Only three regiments — Guards and line Dragoons—belonged to the regular cavalry, of which two (51st and 52nd Dragoons) only arrived with the 17th Army Corps at the theatre of war at the end of July, 1904.

The 4th Division of Don Cossacks arrived still later at the field army—the end of October, 1904.

Of the Orenburg, Ural, and different Asiatic Cossack organizations, which formed the main body of the Russian cavalry in Manchuria, more than half consisted of troops of the second and third class of reserves.

The disillusion, which the activity of the Russian cavalry in general has prepared, must to a great extent be put to the charge of these irregular Cossack corps.

Even before the outbreak of the campaign, in foreign military circles it was no longer any secret that the Don Cossack regiments, which were apportioned to the European cavalry divisions, at most only answered half the requirements of modern cavalry.

For years a perceptible want of horses has made itself felt in all Cossack districts.

The men who were coming up to serve, and whose duty it was from time immemorial to bring horses and weapons with them, had not been for a long time in a position to comply with this demand. Remount duty had, therefore, to be taken over by the Government. Owing to this there were such difficulties to overcome that the mounting of the Cossack troops, especially those of the second and third class of reserves, left very much to be desired. The normal establishment was seldom or ever really attained.

The want of horses, the insufficient pay, the increased demands for military efficiency, probably conduced to make unpopular a service which formerly was considered especially honourable. The seething discontent which was present in the whole of the Russian Empire had penetrated to the steppes of the Don, the Urals, and the Volga.

Many people avoided military service. Desertion in Cossack regiments was quite an everyday occurrence.

Also, the officers of these troops were quite incapable of raising the deteriorating spirit of their men.

Among all his comrades in the huge army of the Czar, the Cossack officer stands morally and intellectually on the lowest rung.

In this respect little superior to his men, in general he is united to them in a good patriarchal relationship. Nevertheless, he is not suited to be a shining example and pattern, which is able to call forth self-sacrificing deeds in difficult positions.

When the insufficient performances of the

Cossack troops made themselves uncomfortably felt at the commencement of the campaign, the War Office determined, as a means of raising the quality of their officers, to transfer a great number of cavalry officers of the Guard to them.

In personal intelligence, courage, and initiative, it is certain that these gentlemen were not lacking. But in service experience, and, above all, in appreciation of the peculiarities of their new subordinates, they left much to be desired.

Their appearance at the front, therefore, had no appreciable influence on the usefulness of the Russian cavalry.

Improvisation is nowhere so useless as by the cavalry arm. This arm must be exactly equipped in peace as one expects to use it in war.

Of the higher leaders which fate placed at the head of the Russian cavalry during the war in the Far East one can give a decidedly better testimony than that placed to the account of their subordinates. Especially in Rennenkampf is the stuff of which an excellent cavalry leader is made.

Even Mischtschenko and Ssamsonow would probably have shown themselves in a more advantageous light provided the material they had to work with had been better.

Indeed, they enjoyed the confidence of their troops, but knew their weaknesses too well to engage in bold and independent enterprises. The few really clearly defined strategical tasks which were given the cavalry leaders by the chief of the army were, however, adequately solved—thus, the guarding of the passes in the Fönschuiling Mountains against the armies of Kuroki and Nodzu ; the guarding of the flanks of their own army at Liaoyang (Kuroki's crossing over and outflanking movement was reported at the right time to Kuropatkin by the brigade of Dragoons of the 17th Army Corps) ; and, finally, Rennenkampf's raid against the extreme right wing of the Japanese at Bönsihu in the battle of Yentai‑Shaho.

What confidence the Russian commander had in the last-mentioned cavalry leader is shown best by the fact that at Mukden he transferred him as quickly as possible from the right wing to the left as an independent commander, immediately the attack of the Japanese seemed to be directed on that wing.

In one respect, however, we can draw a conclusion from the deeds of the Russian cavalry, deficient as are their records up to date. The fault for the sins of omissions—that many such were committed there is absolutely no doubt—are not to be attributed entirely to the leadership, but also to the troops themselves.

Most difficult of all is it to give an exhaustive and just answer to the very interesting and important question : " Has the Russian cavalry carried out to the full its duties and obligations in the service of reconnaissance ?" Our own peace experiences alone ought to prevent us from giving here a too hasty judgment.

To foreign opinions one should not give a too unqualified belief before the Russian cavalry itself has spoken in its own justification.

What the arm performs in reconnaissance is a series of small moves, which form the basis for the important resolves and decisions.

Should fortune favour their own army, the difficult detail work which has been performed by the cavalry will be forgotten in the genius of the commander and the deeds of valour of the other arms on the battlefield. On the other hand, if the tide of events go against it, one is only too inclined to make a scapegoat of the cavalry for its insufficient or negative reports.

As far as concerns the Russian cavalry, it has to defend itself against an indictment emanating from a very important quarter. In a general order, published shortly after the battle of Liaoyang, General Kuropatkin accuses the arm " of having left him in ignorance of the numbers and **intentions** of the enemy." A few critics, doubtless biassed by this and similar judgments, have seen fit to lay the blame for the defeat at Mukden to a great extent on the shoulders of the cavalry which was apportioned to the westerly wing of the Russian army.

They are said not to have reported the great turning movement of the 3rd Japanese Army under General Nogi.

If this is the case, it is without doubt a too inexcusable crime. Not to discover, in a completely open country, three and a half infantry divisions, with numerous artillery, of the advancing enemy the cavalry must have been indeed struck with blindness.

To the honour of the whole cavalry be it said, such a monstrous case in reality never took place.

On February 27th—that is, one day after the commencement of the turning movement—the presence of a strong Japanese force of infantry at Tawan, on the Liaoho (the left-wheeling wing of Nogi's army), was ascertained by the Caucasian cavalry brigade, and duly reported. Cossack patrols also reported the occupation of Sinmintins by the Japanese cavalry, whereupon the mixed Russian brigade of Bürger was sent in that direction.

It is therefore inadmissible to saddle the cavalry of the Russian west wing with the responsibility for the mischief which was caused by the turning movement of the Japanese. By a more correct grouping of his forces (shorter, more massed front, strong reserves well in rear) it would have been easily possible for Kuropatkin to make the necessary dispositions in plenty of time for a successful defence, in accordance with the reports which were received.

However, this does not alter the fact that, in our opinion, the Russian commander could and ought to have been better served here.

Not only the advance, but the preparations for Nogi's movement behind the left wing of the enemy, should have been discovered and reported a long time before. The great weakness of the enemy's cavalry, and the shallowness of the Japanese front, considerably lightened this task.

A strategical reconnaissance in the cavalry sense, with contact patrols and detachments pushed well out to the front, appears neither immediately before the battle of Mukden, nor at any time on the part of the Russians, to have taken place. No such reproach can be levelled against the Japanese cavalry. Their own leaders were always informed well and correctly about the movements of the Russians.

In lay circles to-day one is still inclined to ascribe the merit of this fact exclusively to a widespreading, well-organized system of espionage. In our opinion, the reputation of the Japanese cavalry unjustly suffers through this assumption.

That at times important news through especially clever spies may have been brought in is not to be denied. But to keep the chiefs of the army continuously and reliably informed of the operations of the Russians, it is impossible that the intelligence of the material of which the Chinese spies were composed could have sufficed. Without a correct eye for tactics and a certain constructive talent it is impossible to perform such a service for any length of time.

In the service of reconnaissance it is not only in their self-sacrificing devotion to duty, but, above all, in their intellectual qualities, that the Japanese cavalry have won their greatest triumph. On the other hand, the performances of the Cossacks in the service of reconnaissance were essentially impaired by the low average mental standard of this force.

By a comparison of the relative strength of the two cavalries in the Manchurian theatre of war, owing to the enormous superiority of the Russians, a double reproach must be levelled against them—firstly, that in many cases they saw too little; secondly, that they did not sufficiently hinder their weak opponent from seeing.

In order to prevent any misunderstandings, we will at once solemnly state that we are in no way upholders of the so-called screen tactics in the sense in which so many imagine as being the chief rôle of cavalry. Viewed in the current manner, this duty contains an avowed defensive and passive character quite contrary to the spirit of the arm.

Quite irrespective of this, the idea of a thin cavalry screen surrounding their own army, either on the march or in camp, for protection against view of the enemy, is very fallacious. An energetic enemy, full of enterprise, will easily pierce this thin web with his scouts. Only an active screen can be of any use, which really, in practice, is no longer a screen only, but is coincident with the true offensive reconnaissance.

He who advances regardlessly into the hostile reconnaissance zone, and attacks the cavalry detachments of the enemy with determination wherever they are found, gives the death-blow to the information apparatus of the enemy. His patrols and detachments, robbed of their supports, are soon useless. They, like their reports, only in the fewest cases are able to reach their destination.

At any rate, one can give certain excuses for the Russian cavalry divisions having never used an active screen. The mountainous and roadless character of the country in a great part of the theatre of war, and also the roads in the plains, during a great part of the year covered either with deep mud or with snow and ice, were little favourable to a bold decisive advance. Another thing is, the Japanese cavalry seldom committed themselves willingly to shock tactics, but chose for defence dismounted action, at the same time assuring themselves in a cautious manner always

2

good positions and, generally, the support of their own infantry.

Frequently, however, the Russian squadrons were quite strong enough not to let slip the opportunity of attacking the few companies or even battalions of the mixed Japanese reconnoitring detachments.

With justice the Hungarian Honved-Hussar, Captain Spaits, in his highly interesting book, *With the Cossacks in Manchuria,* specially in connexion with the psychology of this memorable war, says : " Besides military training, above all, the Russian cavalry failed in the firm resolve to sacrifice themselves, and perhaps this was their greatest fault." Even the manner in which the cavalry of Kuropatkin used the long pauses in the operations, which were characteristic of the campaign in Manchuria, did not show that fervid activity which should always be one of the chief attributes of the arm. Neither the losses which they suffered in the three great battles nor any other circumstances can justify the complete inactivity of the Russian cavalry during the months of September, November, and December, 1904, and further in April, May, June, and July, 1905.

Immediately after the days of Liaoyang, at which time it can be accepted that a certain amount of disorder prevailed on the Japanese lines of communication, and that no attack on them was expected, this was, in our opinion, the time to carry out a great raid against the stretch of railway Liaoyang–Haitschön.

At that time the roads were still passable, even if the crossing of the not yet frozen river courses had demanded a certain amount of time and trouble. However, the suddenness of the movement, on which, in the first place, the success of a raid is dependent, should have been taken into account at this period instead of in January, when it was at last resolved to make an effort.

It is certain that to General Kuropatkin one must give a certain amount of the blame for the long inactivity of his squadrons. Should the necessary initiative fail them, then the Commander-in-Chief must give the necessary impulse. Finally, at any rate, by his orders the great raid of General Mischtschenko was let loose.

We must notice that the above-mentioned order, in only containing the general instruction to carry out a raid in rear of the Japanese army, was perfectly correct. The time, as well as the manner of carrying it out, was left to the discretion of General Mischtschenko. The forces placed at his command were ample. Sixty-six squadrons, five and two-thirds batteries, four machine-guns, and four companies of mounted infantry (selected from different infantry regiments), assembled on January 8th at 1 p.m. at Sukudiapu, 20 kilometres south-west of Mukden, to start out on their ride under the command of their popular cavalry leader.

An engineer detachment, a pontoon-bridge detachment, and four sotnias of mounted Frontier Guards were added to it. The best cavalry regiments of the Russian Manchurian army— three regiments of Don Cossacks and three of dragoons—belonged to the raiding corps, a circumstance which must not be overlooked when judging of the performances of Mischtschenko. The leader of every military operation must have some definite objective in his mind's eye, the attainment of which he must in the first instance strive after.

This, without doubt, holds good for cavalry raids, only with this difference—that here an undeviating adherence to the intention which is once formed must in no way be made the rule.

A cavalry raiding force should occasion as much loss as possible to the enemy by means of unpleasant surprises.

The where and how is immaterial. If it does not succeed by the means at first projected, well then, the leader must possess a mind of fertile resource, and try and carry it out in some other way. The principal thing, however, is to appear as unexpectedly as possible on the flanks and rear of the enemy, and to be a nuisance to him as long as is feasible.

It cannot be maintained that General Mischtschenko, either in the planning or execution of his raid, took into consideration these principles.

His plan, in the first instance, was to fall upon
the Japanese depot of Inkau (since the harbour
there was frozen over—this the Russian cavalry
General appears to have been unaware of—the
whole of the enemy's supplies went by Dalny).
The destruction of the railway-line Port Arthur–
Liaoyang appeared to him only a matter of minor
consideration.

These two ideas ought to have been decidedly
looked at the other way about. It was exactly
the above-mentioned railway which was the weak
point of the Japanese, from which it ought to
have been presumed that the transport of Nogi's
army to the north was going forward at this time.

The unfavourableness of the country—roads
covered with slippery ice, and hard, frozen
ploughed fields—was indeed a fact to be deplored,
but, at the same time, not to be altered. So much
the more ought General Mischtschenko to have
taken care on account of this to avoid anything
which would hinder the quick advance of his
troops, one of the most essential factors to success.

From this point of view, the taking with him
1,600 baggage animals for the conveyance of
provisions was a great mistake, for which he paid
a corre·ponding penalty.

During a raid the cavalry must live on the
country, or, still better, from the rations which
they are able to take from the enemy. In the
cultivated, rich plain to the west of the railway-line

Haitschön–Liaoyang the first, at least, was quite possible. With the exception of the ammunition-waggons, during such an undertaking no wheeled transport of any sort should be taken. Notwithstanding the fact that the Russian advance was hindered by bands of Chunchuses and small Japanese infantry detachments (half a company, which had occupied a small trench, kept back Mischtschenko's middle column, more than a division strong, three hours at Kiliho), and proceeded very slowly (average march 29 kilometres daily), when they arrived before Niutschwang about noon on January 12th, the situation was not at all unfavourable.

It was without doubt possible to advance during the same day direct on Haitschön, which was supposed to be occupied by 1,500 Japanese, artillery and infantry.

Eight thousand five hundred sabres with thirty-four guns certainly ought to have risked an attack on this weak force. If Haitschön fell into the hands of the Russians, and if the railway-line, together with the bridges, had been destroyed, a brilliant success would have been obtained.

But even if one wished to avoid the losses which the capture of a fortified place would have entailed, at least Mischtschenko's columns should have been pushed forward against other places as far as the railway, for the more successful destruction of the same. Instead of which, keeping to his original plan, the side-issue to Inkau was undertaken. The railway-station was successfully stormed by twelve dismounted sotnias of Cossacks (all from different regiments), and several buildings and magazines were burnt to the ground.

Meanwhile, on the railway - lines Inkau–Daschitsao and Daschitsao–Haitschön strong officer patrols carried out some inconsiderable demolitions.

These were the entire results which were carried out on this raid by such considerable forces. The Russians did not dare to attack Inkau in the dark, so that the two Japanese militia battalions which garrisoned it were left in undisturbed possession.

The sudden retreat of Mischtschenko—really owing to the report that different hostile infantry columns were advancing direct on them—cannot be looked upon by the critic as satisfactory.

In this open neighbourhood there could be no question of cutting off their retreat.

They had decidedly up to this time performed too little to leave the country in rear of the enemy.

It is maintained (a foreign attaché who accompanied the raid is Captain Spait's authority) that General Mischtschenko wished to spare his troops for the battle of Sandepu, and, in order to take part in this battle, wished to arrive in his own lines in time.

Such reservations are no good; they only prevent the leader from putting his whole soul and spirit into the business in hand.

If one puts aside the fact of the severe winter cold and the slippery ice, the conditions were without doubt specially favourable for Mischt-schenko's raid. He had before him a long, sensitive, and weakly occupied hostile line of communications, the road to which led through an open, cultivated country with rich resources. Defiles, by which the advance could be stopped or the retreat endangered, were non-existent, and, last but not least, the hostile cavalry as a factor in the situation—in the face of his own strength—had not to be reckoned with.

It is a great pity that this opportunity was not made better use of to refresh the—alas !—rather fading laurel crown of the cavalry arm.

It was not only during the pauses between the operations, but also during the days and weeks of the great decisive battles, that the Russian cavalry showed no desire for action in which we recognize the first and most important attribute of our arm.

On the other hand, a just critic, without any further ado, must admit that the prevailing conditions made it extraordinarily difficult for the cavalry masses of Kuropatkin to play the part of cavalry in battle. Indeed, we do not mind openly declaring that, in our opinion, no other

European cavalry, supported by the principles of the cavalry tactics of the day, would have been in a position to perform anything of note on the Manchurian battlefields.

Every sensible cavalryman willingly allows that the time for an attack in masses on infantry which is still in the hand of their leaders is past.

In the campaign of 1870-1871 such death rides were risked by several self-sacrificing squadrons—*i.e.*, Bredow's brigade, Reichshoffen Cuirassiers, and Margueritte's division at Sedan. But since the battlefield has been ruled by the magazine rifle, and now with the spade as an ally, such attempts are not to be thought of for one instant.

A possible object of attack will be offered the victorious cavalry only on infantry which have been wearied by a pursuing fire, and which have been driven out of their positions in disorder. As long as the two battle fronts are struggling with one another the cavalry arm is obliged to respect, unrestrained, the emptiness of the modern battlefield. As the lion-hearted Japanese infantry never gave the Russian dragoons or Cossacks the pleasure of retreating in disorder in order to exemplify the last-mentioned principles, it remained only for the latter to seek out the hostile cavalry. This also the Russian cavalry divisions did not succeed in doing—whether through their own fault remains for the present undecided. At Wafangku the mixed division of Simonow and the 1st Japanese cavalry brigade of Akijama were on opposite wings.

At Liaoyang we find on the west wing of the Russians two and a half cavalry divisions (Ssamsonow, Grekow, and Mischtschenko's brigade).

Curiously enough, one of them (Ssamsonow) was kept far back in the rear in the second line of defence. However, it was quite possible for the senior cavalry General to have united the above-mentioned forces on August 29th for combined operation. What this operation should have been we reserve to ourselves to discuss more minutely later on.

The opportunity which was lost at Liaoyang of performing something on the battlefields did not present itself to the Russian cavalry in such a favourable manner during the later phases of the campaign. Neither on the Shaho, nor at Mukden, did the dispositions of the Commander-in-Chief allow them to appear in such strength at one point in the battle front. In both engagements their force was so ingeniously scattered that it would have required unusual energy and initiative on the part of the cavalry leaders to perform anything with their arm.

So we find that, during the advance against the Japanese positions at the beginning of October, 1904 (battle of Yenkai-Shaho), the Orenburg Cossack division of Grekow was on the extreme right wing on the Liacho; both Mischtschenko's brigades were in the centre with General Mau's connecting detachment; the Siberian Cossack division of Ssamsonow was on the east wing under Stackelberg; and, finally, the Transbaikal Cossack division of Rennenkampf, with a mixed brigade of infantry, was employed as an independent group on a wide turning movement against the Japanese right flank on the upper Tai-tseho. Thus, of the 149 squadrons of the Russian field army, at no point on the battle front were more than 24 available for combined action.

The grouping of the forces by the Commander-in-Chief at the battle of Mukden was nearly as great a sin against the cavalry arm as at the battle on the Shaho.

Only with the Western Detachment was there a solid body of 36 squadrons (at first under General Rennenkampf, consisting of the Ural–Transbaikal–Cossack division and the Caucasian cavalry brigade). The remainder of the great cavalry force was again split up along the battle front. The 17th Army Corps in the centre, and the 3rd Siberian Corps on the left wing, had been provided with a strong corps of cavalry—quite out of proportion to their strength; for what reason it is hard to discover.

The former had a brigade of dragoons, and the latter 18 sotnias of Siberian Cossacks.

Forty-one squadrons more we find distributed among the remaining infantry, and, finally, 16 sotnias of Transbaikal Cossacks with Alexejew's force (later Rennenkampf's).

The whole division of Don Cossacks was ordered far away to the north for the protection of the railway, therefore it has nothing to do with the battle of Mukden.

But the thirty-six squadrons on the extreme right wing of the Russians represent always a force which, in some way or other, should have made their presence felt during the decisive battles which took place there. After the transfer of Rennenkampf to the eastern wing they appear, however, to have been neither well handled nor employed for united action. All we discover about them is that they were constantly driven back by the weak Japanese cavalry division (16 squadrons), and that they neither prevented the capture of Sinmintin nor the successful attack on their own brigade of Bürger.

The behaviour of the Russian cavalry at Mukden leaves one with the impression that their power of fighting had suffered considerably through the battles and fatigues which they had already gone through.

The extraordinary weak condition—scarcely 100 men per squadron—with which they commenced this battle appears to justify the acceptance of this view.

May certain authorities of our army recognize here an exhortation not to assess too low the untiring peace activity of our brave and able regimental squadron commanders! That which these industrious men promote and produce— *i.e.*, order, discipline, well-trained horses, good riders who possess the cavalry spirit and love for their horses—these are the factors which alone in war assure the fighting virtues of the cavalry arm.

The right undoubtedly belongs to the Russian cavalry, with whose battle performances we have declared ourselves not at all in agreement (allowing, however, extenuating circumstances), to put to us this question : " Well, then, how ought we to have done it ?"

We can give an answer short and to the point : A bold offensive in every case in which they were given the duty of protecting the flanks of their own army.

A cavalry corps of several divisions—as many as this could have been combined at Liaoyang, on the Shaho, and on the westerly wing at Mukden; and if it was not done, then the Commander-in-Chief of the army was to be blamed— has no business to remain passive and waiting until it suits the enemy to attack or turn the flank which it is their duty to guard. Otherwise it degrades itself to the level of an ordinary contact patrol. If the enemy does not come, then they have performed nothing ; if he appears, then, in the face of his masses of infantry, there is nothing left but to retreat.

It appears to be far more correct to accept the adage that "prevention is better than cure," and to solve the duty of protecting the flanks by one's self gaining the flanks and rear of the opposing enemy.

Naturally, this must be done by taking in a sufficiently large extent of ground to meet the corresponding conditions, and at the same time sending out patrols far away in all directions.

The principal thing is that the cavalry divisions, provided with machine-guns, horse artillery, and all other technical resources, should be conscious of their strength, and should scorn to rely constantly on their own infantry for support.

Being entirely "on their own" should in no way embarrass a cavalry corps.

The army of Nogi operated at Mukden ten to twelve days separated from their base.

So much the more must an independent cavalry do this during a " battle raid " (*Schlachtenraid*), as we here suggest, throughout a few days.

If the enemy intends an enveloping or turning movement on the flank, which we ride round in the manner in which we have already mentioned, then we meet his columns half-way.

One's own army hears of the threatening danger in time to make the necessary dispositions for defence. Our cavalry, cleverly handled, will find the opportunity to make a flank attack on the enemy himself. This should undoubtedly have taken place by the eighty to ninety Russian squadrons which could have been concentrated at Mukden on the western flank.

It was their duty to hang on like a bull-dog to the left wing of the Japanese turning army, in order to make their march as hard as possible in every conceivable manner. We have not in our mind's eye, it goes without saying, attacks with the *arme blanche* as the most suitable means, but the making use to the utmost of our mobility and of the ground ; to appear suddenly again and again, and to disappear as suddenly ; to be always first where the fire effect of carbines, machine-guns, and horse artillery could be used with the greatest execution.

Having once gained touch with the enemy, he should never have a chance of rest again. Exhaust him, and make his advance slower—in any case, become like a gnat to him, and at times give him hornet stings.

A manœuvre like that we have just described, the Russian cavalry could naturally only play at Mukden after they had completely beaten the Japanese cavalry division out of the field.

By their great superiority of numbers this was in no way a difficult task.

For the operations which we have here proposed it is, of course, an essential condition that we should have obtained a decisive victory over the hostile cavalry which was to be met with on this battle wing. This is, above all, the first thing to be aimed at. To attain this we must be able to everlastingly gallop, attack with determination, and use our weapons with effect.

If the "battle raid" of a cavalry corps does not meet with the advancing hostile forces, then it must be pushed, well spread out, right in the rear of the enemy's fighting-line.

To see the opposing reserves having to advance into action is already something achieved.

From the moment that the force has successfully reached the rear of the enemy's lines the greatest demands on the power of judgment and resolution are required of the leader.

It then rests with him to decide when the moment for an attack, regardless of all consequences, has arrived. It is only in the fewest cases that his own commander is in a position to inform him of what is going on, and to cause him to attack at the right time, in spite of the best-organized service of information, telephone, wireless telegraphy, and flag-signalling.

In his isolated position, he will therefore, as a general rule, have to discern from the most scanty signs, but with a fine tactical instinct, the near approach of the crisis.

If it appears that this turns against the enemy, it is his line of retreat which is the magnet by which our cavalry corps should be irresistibly attracted.

Towards the end of the battle of Mukden (about evening of March 9th, 1905) the Japanese cavalry found themselves in just such a favourable situation.

Unfortunately, they proved unequal to the task (was it weariness ? was it the breakdown of their horses ?) and were prevented from so acting. Later we shall return to this interesting episode.

On the other hand, should the decisive attack decide in favour of the hostile army, then it becomes the duty of our cavalry divisions, who will have pressed forward to the rear of the enemy, to prevent and hinder to the utmost the advance of the hostile reserves to complete the victory. On August 31st, 1904, between the hours of seven and eight in the evening, the attack, with the aid of the last troops intact (three reserve brigades) of the 2nd and 4th Japanese armies on the principal lines of defence south of Liaoyang, failed.

Terribly decimated and totally exhausted, the storming columns of Generals Oku and Nogi retreated to their own positions.

We have already seen that a Russian cavalry corps of three divisions could have easily been concentrated on their own extreme right wing at the beginning of the battle.

If this mounted mass had employed the days of August 28th to the 31st to ride round the hostile wing in a large arc to reach the railway-line somewhere in the neighbourhood of Shaho Station, they

3

could have employed the moment just described in an attack on the retreating hostile infantry.

Whether here a decisive success was to be obtained against the Japanese infantry one cannot say. At any rate, the situation quite justified the attempt of winning honour once again for the *arme blanche*. If the attack had succeeded, then Oku could certainly not have carried out his attack during the night. And it is hardly likely that Kuroki's weak turning movement on the east flank would have caused Kuropatkin to give up his south front. Liaoyang would have been a defeat for the Japanese.

In like manner, in the last stages of the battle on the Shaho, we are convinced that an enterprising Russian cavalry leader would certainly have found the opportunity in rear of the Japanese for a successful attack on the thin hostile lines, which were tired to death owing to the battle which had lasted day and night. However, we do not in any way maintain that the activity of the Russian cavalry ought to have been developed exactly in the manner in which we have indicated ; for that the details of the different fights are much too meagre.

Concerning the " when," " how," and " where," one can certainly still argue. On the other hand, it is certain that such considerable cavalry masses ought to have done something to relieve their infantry and artillery during the decisive battles.

As this did not take place on any single occasion, Kuropatkin's cavalry cannot remain free of the reproach that they entirely failed in the necessary spirit of self-sacrifice. This does not at all mean that for this failure the troops themselves alone were answerable. They would have in all probability willingly done what was required of them. The dislike of risking a big stake—a characteristic of the whole Russian leadership in the Far East— had worked its infection from above, and also influenced strongly the operations of the cavalry.

The few praiseworthy exceptions to the general inactivity of the Russian cavalry are bound up with the name of General Rennenkampf.

In the battle of Yentai–Shaho he led his detachment (24 squadrons, 16 battalions, 8 batteries) with remarkable enterprise over the mountain passes against the Japanese communications on the upper Tai-tse-ho. For days he energetically attacked there the hostile positions in front of Bönsiku.

The tough defence of the opposing Japanese reserve brigades, reinforced by the cavalry brigade of Kanin, and the ill-success of the remaining Russian columns, compelled him, notwithstanding the fact he had done his utmost, to retreat. Wherever he commanded, something, at least, was always done. After the battle of Sandepu he took over command of the Russian Western Division in the place of the wounded General Mischtschenko.

In the middle of February, shortly before the battle of Mukden, he started on a raid upon Liaoyang, in the rear of the Japanese, with the thirty-six squadrons which he had available.

Unfortunately, the details of this operation are still considerably shrouded in obscurity. Most of the historians of the campaign pass it over in complete silence.

We obtain our knowledge of this event from the book of the Royal Hungarian Honved-Hussar, Captain Spait, which we have favourably mentioned before.

Without doubt certainly more would have been heard about the cavalry of the Russian west wing if Rennenkampf had not been taken suddenly, during the first phases of the debacle at Mukden, to command the Eastern Army, which Kuropatkin considered to be especially threatened.

Likewise here we see signs of his inspiriting influence. Immediately after his arrival his eighteen sotnias of Transbaikal Cossacks carried out an offensive reconnaissance to ascertain exactly the extent of the Japanese attacking front. As a respectable performance of the Russian cavalry the defence of the coal-mines of Yentai during the battle of Liaoyang is worthy of notice.

The Siberian Cossacks of Ssamsonow's Corps, through their fire, brought to a halt the Japanese, who were pressing on after the defeated division of Orlow.

These scanty specks of light on a dark background, which we have here given at the end for the purpose of having as propitious a close as possible to our rather sad tale of the inactivity of the Russian cavalry during the campaign, may be supplemented at a future time from data not yet to hand.

But it is certain that the whole picture, which we have described here in its outlines, cannot to any great extent be altered.

(b) THE JAPANESE.

Provided with insufficient means, a great task was given the Japanese cavalry in the war in the Far East.

Although the cavalry did its very best to solve that task, it cannot, of course, satisfy an impartial critic.

Also the Japanese cavalry arm has had to suffer frequently from the common talk about its complete fiasco in the latest campaign. Too weak and badly mounted to engage in brilliant attacks against the hostile squadrons, or to prepare a disaster for the retreating hostile hosts, it had to confine itself to more modest performances.

The faithful carrying out of their duty in small affairs is, however, completely put into the shade by the brilliant fame which has been won by the other arms of the Japanese army.

We would like to bring to the remembrance of those gentlemen, the critics, who find no word of recognition for these brave men, who were so badly equipped by their own Government, the general prognostication which was current in military circles at the commencement of the campaign : " The Japanese cavalry, which are of little use, will be simply swept out of the field by the Russian cavalry masses " ; and, further : " The Japanese commander will, on this account, be in a very bad position. Reliable information will fail him about his opponent, and his communications will be continually cut." Nothing of this sort, however, occurred. The Japanese Generals were always completely informed of the movement of the Russians; their cavalry maintained the field, and, in spite of their weakness, always kept touch with their opponents. Their own line of communications enjoyed, for the most part, perfect security. The inactivity of the Russian cavalry is chiefly to blame that the course of events took such a favourable turn for the Japanese mounted troops.

However, without able and bold leadership in the face of the superior numbers of their opponents, they would never have succeeded in developing such a useful reconnoitring activity. In another place we have already mentioned that the Japanese leaders, for the best of their information, had to thank, without doubt, the reconnaissances of their cavalry, and not, as is generally believed in lay circles, their Chinese spies. " Intelligence and an absolute contempt of death," so says a prominent historian of the latest war (Major Immanuel of the Prussian General Staff), " are the qualities mostly required of the modern soldier."

Now, the Japanese cavalryman possessed these in as full a measure as his comrades of the other arms ; and, therefore, he has proved himself to be an excellent scout and dispatch rider in spite of his want of good horsemanship and his slow and badly trained horse.

In every Japanese soldier—the cavalryman included—existed the firm determination to conquer, cost what it might. This spirit admitted of no inactivity, but, on the contrary, produced an overpowering eagerness for the offensive. As we shall see, the latter found expression in the cavalry, as far as it lay within their power.

From this let us obtain this maxim, which we justly consider one of the advantages of our organization, training, and horse material—never to neglect to foster the moral elements and spirit of our men. For, in the end, it is these factors, be it either in the cavalry charge, infantry fight, or artillery duel, which will be decisive.

The cavalryman who takes the trouble to follow attentively that which the Japanese cavalry performed in a small way will experience a sincere regret that they did not enter the campaign better equipped.

If this had been the case, they are certain, following the example of their indomitable infantry, to have resuscitated the dead-letter of our cavalry drill-books to a living truth. Then, perhaps, we could with the more certainty maintain, given a brave heart and a strong arm, that the era of the sword, as well as that of the bayonet, is not passed.

It appears to a certain extent strange that the administrators of the modern Japanese army, who otherwise, in every other particular, may be so proud of their work, dealt in such a niggardly manner with the cavalry arm.

Perhaps it was that they did not foresee that Japan within a few decades would have to measure her strength against an opponent who had a mighty cavalry at his disposal on the, generally speaking, level fields of Manchuria.

It is for this reason only that one can understand the neglect of a strong, well-mounted cavalry. Indeed, the conditions in Japan for the use of this arm are highly unfavourable: a pathless, mountainous country on the one hand, on the other an extremely highly cultivated country, allow them scarcely any freedom of movement.

The breeding of animals is everywhere but little developed in the Island Kingdom.

Quite irrespective of the difficulty to provide

extensive grazing-ground in this overcultivated country, the strongly-salted land produces but a very indifferent green fodder. Even before the war the extraordinarily weak Japanese cavalry could not be provided with the necessary horses home-bred, but had to be mounted almost entirely on Australian ponies little suited to cavalry work.

The creation of a strong and modern cavalry arm presents, by the further increase of the Japanese forces, the first and most difficult problem.

Under all circumstances a solution must be found. The experiences of the battle of Mukden alone prove this to be essential. There was only wanted here a few cavalry divisions to gather the completely ripe fruits from the tree, which the infantry, tired to death, were unable to reap.

A peace such as the Japanese nation wished and deserved would probably have been the result of an energetic cavalry pursuit.

Eyewitnesses (Captain Spait amongst others) of the retreat of the 2nd and 3rd Russian armies, which took place in the greatest disorder, entirely confirm this view.

As it is a question of laying the necessary foundations for the reorganization of the cavalry, now as good as non-existent, it is imperative to advise the Japanese Government to dispatch a number of officers to Austria, Germany, and France to study the remount question.

Above all, provincial attempts must be made

to improve the quality of the native horse by means of judicious crossings. Without consideration of the cost, they should build at once the necessary number of runs for mares and foals to bring the native horses, not only in quality but in quantity, to the necessary standard.

As the Japanese, in a physical respect, are little adapted to riding, and as, therefore, the cavalry recruit should undergo a specially careful training, they should not hesitate, even after the victories they have won, to call in a number of prominent foreign cavalry officers as instructors. In spite of the various valiant deeds which the Japanese cavalry carried out during the course of the campaign, they failed to a great extent in the correct technical employment of the arm.

By this means only can performances which will influence a campaign be carried out by the arm.

In the interest of the cavalry student it is much to be regretted that, neither on the side of the Russians nor that of the Japanese, is any record kept of the number of the horses which, in the course of the campaign, were rendered unfit for service.

One will not be far wrong when one places the numbers on both sides as very considerable ; for the Japanese cavalry also are said to have saddled, bitted, and looked after their animals badly. At the commencement of the campaign Japan had at disposal one guard and sixteen line cavalry regiments. The former carried, besides the sword and carbine, the lance, which, however, was left at home.

Each of the thirteen infantry divisions had apportioned to them as divisional cavalry one regiment of three squadrons. The cavalry regiments of the line, Nos. 13, 14, 15, and 16, each consisting of four squadrons, formed two independent cavalry brigades.

In the battle of Mukden these, which formerly had been apportioned to different armies, were formed into a division. The reserve infantry brigades (divisions) which were formed later had at disposal only a reserve squadron.

In consideration of the great want of cavalry, the head-quarter staff of the Japanese army, by the apportionment of a whole cavalry regiment to each infantry division of the field army, committed an act of great waste.

It would have been decidedly preferable to employ only one or two squadrons for this purpose. Then, instead of only two, at least twice that number of independent cavalry brigades could have been formed, which, concentrated, would have been far more able to carry out a great strategical or tactical task.

Thus it is that the Japanese cavalry only undertook one single raid at any distance, and then only with a weak force, which, however, was accompanied with quite phenomenal success.

Shortly before the battle of Mukden two

squadrons succeeded in getting to the rear of the Russians, and partly blowing up the railway-bridge of Guntschuling, which was protected by fortifications.

Resting by day and marching by night, this weak raiding force succeeded in pressing forward quite close to the object without being perceived. Here they dismounted to fire, in order to attract the attention of the garrison at the bridge-head; while a few specially selected men, in spite of the drifting ice, succeeded in reaching the middle arch of the bridge, where they laid the charge. As this exploded, and a great part of the roadway of the bridge flew into the air, both squadrons quickly disappeared in the darkness.

In spite of a zealous pursuit from the enemy, they succeeded in getting safely back to their own troops.

This bold stroke produced a sort of panic in the Russian head-quarters. Kuropatkin became so anxious about his rear communications that, besides the Frontier Guards, which were meant for this duty, he ordered an infantry brigade (2nd of the 41st Division) and the whole of the division of Don Cossacks to the north for the defence of the railway-line.

This brave deed, therefore, of the two squadrons rendered useless during the decisive battle about 8,000 of the best troops of the enemy. Truly a good example in refutation of all those who maintain that the day of cavalry in modern warfare is passed.

As the historian of the campaign has nothing to relate of any other raids of the Japanese cavalry, let us turn to their activity during battle.

On the Yalu and by the storming of the heights of Kiutuscho they did nothing of importance.

On the other hand, the movements of the 1st Independent Cavalry Brigade (Major-General Akijama), before and during the fight at Wafankou, are full of lessons, and very interesting.

As far as we can ascertain from the scant means at our disposal, the leading of this brigade seems to have been a very able one. Sent by General Oku from Pulantien to reconnoitre Wafankou, they carried out, supported by two machine-gun detachments and two infantry battalions, a successful fight against the mixed Russian brigade of Ssamsonow. Here arose a hand-to-hand fight, which in this war seldom took place, and where the lances of the Cossacks are said to have been very useful.

When General Akijama a few days later was driven back by the superior advance guard of Stackelberg, he retreated slowly, still keeping touch with the enemy in a south-easterly direction.

In the battle of Wafankou he appeared on the battlefield just in time (acting on his own initiative) to bring to a standstill the attack of the

2nd Brigade of the 35th Russian Infantry Division (Major-General Glasko).

He thereby freed the 3rd Japanese Division, which stood in imminent danger of having their right flank turned by this hostile advance, from an extremely critical situation.

As the whole east wing of the Russians was obliged, by the general position of the fight, to retreat very soon, the Japanese cavalry brigade pursued energetically, and even drove back the enemy's rear-guard as far as his own fortified position at Tsuitsjatun, carrying this out dismounted, and with quite remarkably small losses.

In the battle on the Shaho the 2nd Independent Cavalry Brigade, under Prince Kotohito-Kanin, helped the weak reserve troops to drive back Rennenkampf's attack on Bönsiku, which was carried out with far superior forces.

At Sandepu the cavalry of Akijama defended this place the whole day against the violent attack of the Russian infantry. It is worthy of notice that they used their blasting cartridges as hand grenades.

At Mukden what the Japanese cavalry actually performed is quite insignificant compared with that which they could have done with stronger forces. But in justice we must say once more that, under the circumstances prevailing, the two independent cavalry brigades of Akijama and Tamura (since March 3rd formed into one weak cavalry division) performed their duty to the best of their ability, also in the decisive battle.

In the first phases of the long fight they pushed forward on the extreme left wing of the Japanese turning army in an extraordinary quick and energetic manner, driving the superior Russian cavalry of the Western Detachment before them. On February 27th Tamura's Brigade had already reached the west bank of the Liaoho at Takou. Their patrols had scouted as far as Sinmintin.

Through this arose the false report of the occupation of this town by a considerable Japanese force, which alarmed the enemy. Kuropatkin dispatched with all possible speed the mixed brigade of Bürger (8 battalions, 1 machine-gun detachment, and 3 batteries), together with the Ural-Transbaikal Cossack Division of the West Army, in this direction.

This force, during the return march from Sinmintin, on March 3rd was surprised by the Japanese cavalry, supported by two battalions, defeated, and cut off from their own army towards the north-east.

On the above-mentioned day the advance-guard of Oyama's cavalry had already reached the railway-line Mukden–Tjelin. From this moment, when it appeared as if they were on the threshold of a great success, their activity almost ceases. The causes are not far to seek. The single cavalry division felt itself too weak to separate itself entirely from Nogi's army, to which it was attached, and to advance alone right away to the north and throw itself against the Russian line of retreat. Besides, Nogi, in his battle order (published on the evening of March 3rd), had expressly entrusted them with the protection of his left flank.

The huge Japanese turning movement which was planned, but in the end carried out with too small a force, resulted, during the days of March 4th to 9th, in a series of the fiercest frontal attacks.

Perhaps the Japanese cavalry, after they had proved themselves to be too weak to carry out the great task which they had hoped—*i.e.*, the prevention of the retreat of the enemy—took part in the above-mentioned fight with the carbine. Anything further about this is not yet known. At any rate, the main body of the Japanese Cavalry Division did not advance any further than to Tasintun up till March 10th (somewhere about 25 kilometres north of Mukden, and 10 kilometres west of the railway-line Mukden–Tjelin).

It is strange that the latter did not seize the opportunity even once, during the Russian retreat which followed, of bombarding from suitable positions the columns which were retreating in disorder.

The single Japanese battery which produced, through a well-directed fire, such a panic in the

Russian transport did not belong to the Cavalry Division.

The Japanese cavalry, as well as their infantry, appeared at this time to have arrived just about at the end of their tether.

What three to four well-mounted, cleverly-led cavalry divisions, equipped with all modern resources, could have accomplished on the side of the Japanese, even the wildest imagination can scarcely conceive.

Even if the detached Russian troops to the north of Mukden—General Kuropatkin himself in the last stages of the battle could not spare another man—had been in a position to prevent the occupation of the defile of Tielin, an energetic pursuit parallel to them must have caused the total dispersion of the 2nd and 3rd Russian armies.

The probable long duration of the battles of the future is, without doubt, a feature which, if properly reckoned with, should prove extraordinarily favourable for the employment of cavalry. It ensures for the cavalry arm the possibility, while preserving to the utmost its own strength for the final act, to approach the point where it wishes its word to be heard in the decision.

The Japanese cavalry, scarcely without exception, carried out their performances with the carbine, and in close touch with their own infantry. To this circumstance, without doubt, we have to

4

ascribe the principal reason why there has been hesitation among military critics in giving full recognition to their activity. A certain narrow-mindedness obstructs the means used to gain the end, which in no way is inclined to further the interests of the arm.

"To be victorious is the chief thing." Under all circumstances this will remain our motto.

If we do not succeed with the sword or lance, then let us try firearms.

If we are too weak to gain success alone, then let us only be too thankful, and accept without scruple the help of our infantry.

Accordingly, on these principles the Japanese cavalry consistently acted.

To reproach them because of this is extremely unjustifiable. Besides, it must not be forgotten that they, as the weakest force, had the manner of fighting dictated to them by their opponents. And one thing more. The irresistible pleasure of charging home with the sword at the quickest pace on an enemy who is cautiously firing from cover will only fall to the lot of that cavalryman who is mounted on a fast-galloping and at the same time manageable horse. This is also the condition which, over ground not too unfavour-able, offers a chance of success to a dashing charge against dismounted cavalry.

One can well offer excuses for the Japanese cavalry, with their slow and stubborn ponies, that they evinced no desire to suffer useless losses, but preferred, following the example of the enemy, to use dismounted fire tactics.

A typical example of the manner in which both cavalries fought in the campaign in the Far East is offered us by the action at Tschöndschu, in Northern Corea (the first of the whole war, on March 28th, 1904).

Six sotnias of Mischtschenko's Cossack Brigade were sent forward from the Yalu to carry out a reconnaissance against Kasan.

As the advance guard — two sotnias — approached the town of Tschöndschu, which, in the manner of the country, was surrounded by a high stone wall, they were suddenly fired upon. Both the squadrons thereupon galloped back in order to dismount behind a suitable hill to use their rifles. The main body meanwhile, coming up, hurried to follow their example with three sotnias. Only one remained mounted in reserve. During this time the Japanese cavalry regiment of the guard from Kasan arrived to reinforce the Japanese pickets which were in Tschöndschu (one squadron and one company of infantry).

This likewise at once dismounted two squadrons on the edge of Tschöndschu for rifle-fire.

The third, which tried to ride round the place, with the intention of prolonging the skirmishing-line, was compelled by the fire of the Cossacks to retire.

After about a two-hour skirmish, which caused few losses (the Russians lost 5 officers and 15 men; the Japanese 3 officers and 17 men in dead and wounded), a Japanese infantry battalion arrived in Tschöndschu at the double. General Mischtschenko now broke off the skirmish, and returned to his former night station, scarcely followed. The behaviour of both cavalry detachments by this first collision of the war may justly surprise us. In no way does it correspond to the spirit which we try to instil into our cavalry. Especially the Russians, who at the commencement were far stronger, whose task it surely was to penetrate as far as possible into the hostile zone of advance, ought certainly not to have allowed themselves to be held at Tschöndschu. That the two advanced sotnias dismounted to fire in order to give their scouts time to reconnoitre the hostile position and ground we may allow to pass. The main body, however, ought not to have hesitated on their arrival to ride round Tschöndschu somehow.

As the town did not lie in a defile, this was certainly possible.

The manœuvre which we have here proposed would have led to a collision with the Japanese cavalry regiment of the guard.

The opportunity to establish cavalry superiority by a dashing attack ought at any price to be sought for during the first fights of a campaign.

That side which maintains the field has afterwards the confidence of victory as a mighty moral factor on its side.

It does not seem beyond the bounds of possibility that if the six Cossack sotnias had obtained a brilliant result against the Japanese cavalry regiment of the guard with the *arme blanche,* the sleeping offensive spirit of the whole Russian cavalry would have been awakened.

To our mind, the Japanese cavalry would have acted more correctly if it had taken advantage of Mischtschenko's mistake in using his whole force for dismounted action by trying a mounted attack against one of the hostile flanks.

The possibility of this manœuvre was, of course, dependent on whether there was somewhere ground over which they could advance unseen again.t the Russian position.

As Tschöndschu is situated in a mountainous district, one can accept the fact that this was the case.

III

CONCLUSIONS

THE course of the reconnoitring fight which
has been described at the end of the last
chapter brings home to us a great question :
Which instinct, taking into consideration the experiences of the late campaign, is the right one for
the cavalryman ?

Should he, on getting a sight of the enemy, put
spurs to his horse, draw his sword from its scabbard and charge, or dismount, take cover and
fire ?

The outspoken impulse in one or other of these
directions must, without doubt, be engendered
during peace-time in the leaders quite as much as
in the men.

At all events, the former should also have learnt
to think, so that, when necessary, the voice of
reason may have a chance of modifying or stifling
the first impulse.

Our cavalry beliefs are in no way altered owing
to the experiences of the war in the Far East.

As formerly, we are convinced that cavalry
which prefers shock action to dismounted action

will carry out the duty incumbent upon it better than where the opposite is the case.

The ideal would perhaps be for them to do each equally willingly—*i.e.*, to be equally efficient with the carbine as with the *arme blanche;* in this we include, besides sword and lance, horsemanship. The attainment of this ideal is, in our opinion, practically impossible. Not only on account of the short service, which scarcely is sufficient to make a man at one and the same time a clever rider, swordsman, and shooter, but also because the sword and the carbine are such different masters that the cavalryman simply cannot serve both with the same love.

It requires quite a different temperament to ride to the attack with drawn sword at the gallop than it does to wait for hours placidly aiming in a fire position.

As long as we lay principal stress on good dashing horsemanship and the clever handling of the *arme blanche*, and relegate training with the rifle to the second place, so long shall we foster the offensive spirit of our cavalry.

On this stands and falls the whole activity of the cavalry arm.

That this is the case was proved sufficiently in the late war by the Russian cavalry, who, it is well known, gave the preponderating care to the training for dismounted action. In a European campaign it will be the first duty of each cavalry to measure its strength with a cavalry of approximately the same strength.

Only after the question is decided by this fight will the victor be able to display a really successful activity in reconnaissance, in raids against the enemy's communications, and, finally, by operations against the flank and rear of the hostile battle front.

The duel between the two cavalries will, without doubt, be in favour of that one who is imbued with the greater offensive spirit.

Cavalry, which seeks its salvation in the rifle, easily loses the impulse to charge home on the enemy.

On the other hand, it is the greatest advantage of the *arme blanche* that this riding home at any price forms the essential *sine qua non* for its use.

Good reconnaissance means to see as much as possible.

That, however, will only be attained through seeking to get to close quarters with the enemy.

The Austro-Hungarian cavalry, owing to their traditions, their excellent mounts, their recruits, who are specially suited for riding, are in an exceptionally favourable position, in our opinion, to choose shock tactics as the preferable means of attack.

In spite of a powerful opposition, principally fostered by the so-called intelligence of the army, our methods of training are still being carried out on these lines.

In our opinion, there is in principle no fault to find with this method.

At the most, a few small working details might be made to agree better with the end in view.

Without detracting in the smallest degree from the training of the horses or the mounted instruction of the men, perhaps it were better if, for example, a few useless figures in the riding-school and on the square were done away with.

More time, by this means, would be gained for more important things.

The exercises for wielding and handling the sword and lance are carried out in too pedantic a manner.

Riding, hours long, with drawn sword, where a uniformity which is scarcely attainable is insisted upon, is, to say the least, quite superfluous. Likewise, pointing at dummies on the ground, and fighting on horseback with masks, uses up more time in accustoming the horses in proportion to the good done for war purposes.

Reliance on the sword and lance, and power and cleverness in their handling, can be just as well taught the man by instruction on foot in all essentials.

Given a good seat and a handy horse, a few lessons on horseback will suffice to teach him the use of the sword mounted.

On the other hand, a man who has no seat or is mounted on an unhandy animal, will practise for hours cutting and pointing in vain.

An obedient, well-balanced horse is the first essential for the proper performance of cavalry duty, whether it be patrol work, attacking, or raiding.   Therefore the breaking of remounts is, and must without doubt always remain, the most important part of individual training.

Our cavalry certainly does its utmost to remain true to this principle.

The very good results which are obtained at the remount schools could certainly be changed for the better by working on a more uniform system. That is unfortunately not yet the case.

Our celebrated regulation concerning the training of young horses, on account of its shortness, is expressed far too laconically.

An addition is decidedly wanted here, together with all the latest principles of horsemanship.

A pronounced influence on the fostering of the noble art of riding should be allowed to its apostles in our arm—*i.e.*, to the officers and sergeants who have been through the military riding institutes.

The justifiable complaint over the ridiculously small peace establishment of our infantry companies becomes always louder ; as far as the cavalry is concerned, the general military opinion seems to be apparently quite satisfied. This arm is, indeed, so they reason (with the exception of the horse for the pay-sergeant), during peace already on a war establishment.

The squadron leader is therefore able to hold

suitable field practices even during the winter with the men of the second and third years' service, as prescribed in the regulations.

This is without doubt extremely necessary. But he who gets a glimpse behind the scenes knows that there is a good deal amiss.

Even under the most favourable circumstances a squadron leader can at the most get only fifty men together for field exercises during the winter months, not counting the recruits.

This is decidedly too small a number to carry out any instructive exercise with the squadron.

In the first place, there is a want of horses. About 64 remounts, 20 still half-trained horses, and 16 horses away in the regimental non-commissioned officers' school, with the pioneer troop, the brigade riding-school, and other institutes, have to be deducted from the 149 which is laid down as the establishment.

Sufficient men to bring the above-mentioned detachment up to 50 fully-trained horsemen are, as a rule, always present, as we all know that the establishment is 171.

However, the great number of men on detached duty for two-thirds of the year (25 to 30 per squadron) forms a great drawback to the efficiency of our cavalry.

As often as the introduction of the two years' service is raised by the representatives of the people, so often from the side of the military is

the objection made that this period is too short
for the proper training of the mounted arm.

But it must be allowed that in reality we of the
cavalry arm can only reckon on a two years'
colour service.

During the months from October to May
generally nearly the whole of the third year's
soldiers are away on detached duty, or absent for
some reason or other from their units—*i.e.*, on
account of leave owing to excess of establishment.

Also in the second year's service it will become
the turn of every man to perform somewhere for
three months mounted orderly or staff service.

It is absolutely necessary to free the squadrons,
if possible, from this vicious system of detailing
men and horses from their squadrons. For this
duty, men transferred last to the reserve and
horses of men on leave should be called up.

For duty with the squadron there should be
at least 70 trained soldiers available at all times.
This is the minimum number with which the
squadron can attempt to do anything worth doing
in the way of drill and training in the open
country. This detailing gave easy-going squadron
leaders hitherto a favourite pretext to excuse the
idling of their old men during winter in the small
manège.

The efficiency of our cavalry would gain much
if the cause for this pretext were done away with.

Before the Russo-Japanese War the possibility

of a winter campaign appeared to us somewhat remote. Now, one will certainly have to reckon with it. What proved itself to be possible in the icy fields of Manchuria is in the European climate certainly much more possible.

That means that in peace-time man and horse should be thoroughly accustomed to the condition of the country and the weather at that rough season of the year.

That this should really be the case, the higher generals should look upon it as their duty to inspect the old soldiers during the winter months, not only in the riding-school, but in the open country as well.

The patrol rules which are laid down are not sufficient for this purpose.

That our cavalry, as soon as they begin to train themselves seriously for the demands of a winter campaign, must, above all, receive suitable clothing, which at present they have not got, goes without saying. We reserve to ourselves to return to this point later on.

By a study of the great raid of General Mischt-schenko at the beginning of January, 1905, the question instinctively forces itself on us, How would a number of Austrian squadrons have stood the same test ?

Now, our conviction is that the answer to most points can be given in a quite satisfactory manner. The advance of our cavalry would have been certainly much faster than that of the Russian, in spite of the ice and frozen ploughed fields.

Our leaders would have, in all probability, grasped the aim of the raid in a much clearer manner than General Mischtschenko. The secondary undertaking against Inkau would not have taken place. Our pioneer troops, properly supported by the main body, would have undoubtedly completely destroyed the railway-line Daschitsao–Haitschön.

The advance of different Japanese infantry columns would not have been the cause of a too early retreat of our squadrons.

Only on one point are we doubtful. How would our men and horses have stood the icy cold of the Manchurian winter nights during the march and in the bivouac ?

Frozen limbs of the men, little inured, and clothed in an unpractical manner, horses suffering from complaints of the respiratory organs, or refusing the fodder, would have to be counted, we fear, in considerable numbers.

It appears not to be beyond the bounds of possibility that our squadrons would have made their appearance at Mukden with still weaker forces than the Russians did.

If we could decide to renounce, in peace-time, the cultivation of round croups and shining summer coats in the winter season, then, without doubt, we should find ourselves in a position to await with greater tranquillity the fatigues of a winter campaign.

The great importance of a proper training for active service has been thoroughly appreciated for some time by our cavalry. We are, of course, somewhat hampered in this by the low standard of education of our men, as well as of a great portion of our non-commissioned officers.

We endeavour to make up for this deficiency by the especially thorough training of our young officers for their duty as leaders of reconnoitring patrols.

That, as far as it goes, is all right, but this decidedly should be extended to the reserve lieutenants and the cadets.

Taking into consideration the fact that, even at the commencement of a war (during the campaign the proportion will become worse), more than half the subalterns' commissions of the field squadrons must be filled up by officers from the reserve, we decidedly behave very much like the ostrich.

The last-named officers come up to serve their twenty-eight days with their units mostly in the months of May and June. Just at this period, when inspections are so many, the squadron leader is fully occupied with training his command to gallop and manœuvre in the short time he is given for that object. No wonder, then, that the much-plagued man does not greet the summer lieutenants with especial joy, or that he does not look upon his task with them in the light of producing an article thoroughly trained.

So that these gentlemen shall spoil nothing (which would be a useless waste of valuable horseflesh), they are allowed to simply trot about the square, or at drill to hack about in the rear.

Joyful exceptions, produced by specially conscientious squadron commanders or by specially suitable reserve officers themselves, it goes without saying there are.

However, as a rule, the thing in practice works out as we have described.

Reserve lieutenants and cadets can only a very few times lead patrols during their service as one-year volunteers and during their later trainings.

This is a want which, in war, may reap its own reward.

It is essentially our cavalry, which has only available a limited number of really intelligent non-commissioned officers, that should especially take care to build up a reserve of officers as useful substitutes for the regular officers in the duty of reconnaissance.

The numbers of the latter are not sufficient, even in the first days of a campaign, for patrol and detachment leaders, much less later on.

An improvement in the present conditions could be obtained by calling up the reserve officers and cadets, as a rule, only during the manœuvres.

During that time the superior officers should take a keen interest in the employment of these gentlemen in the field.

Better that the reserve lieutenants should ride badly in the front and lead a patrol well than it should be the other way about.

It is also highly desirable that the duration of their biennial training should be fixed at eight instead of four weeks for the cavalry, as it is, for example, in Germany.

The greater number of our cavalry reserve officers doubtless have sufficient means not to feel too much the additional burden.

In connexion with the above - mentioned measure, we would propose still further to divide our non-commissioned officers into two strictly separate classes, as far as their usefulness for reconnaissance is concerned.

For the first class—the more intelligent—the demands of a theoretical instruction should be increased ; for the second, on the other hand, they should be essentially decreased. With independent tasks the latter could, anyhow, not be trusted.

The difficulty of cavalry reconnaissance is, as is well known, not so much the art of seeing aright and reporting, but, above all, of sending back at once and safely to the correct place a report of what has been seen.

According to the universal opinion of the

5

different foreign officers who were attached to the Russian cavalry divisions, in this particular it struck them as very bad.

Quite irrespective of the fact that the reports frequently were inaccurate or quite wrong, a great number never reached the hands of the addressees.

In intelligence—partly, also, in the necessary discipline and devotion to duty—the Cossack troops were quite lacking. On the other hand, the Japanese carried out the dispatch duty, like every other, with the greatest keenness and unstinted devotion.

Our cavalry takes a great deal of trouble and care in the training of clever and trustworthy dispatch riders.

In spite of this, in most cavalry regiments it is only a small percentage of the men who acquire the qualification for this most important duty.

He who knows can easily make the observation that, taking, for example, one troop during the manœuvres, it is always the same two or three men who are the deliverers of any really important news.

In the case of verbal reports, if anything, the number of trustworthy men is still more limited.

Modern infantry tacticians are never tired of reiterating how the training of each single skirmisher in independence of thought and action is the first and highest aim of their whole training.

In a still higher degree the cavalry arm has reason to keep this precept in its mind's eye.

Every cavalryman, indeed, may be in the position of having to bring through miles of country occupied by the enemy a report, the arrival of which at the right time might influence the whole course of the war.

Even the best and most zealous schooling would never make a man who is lacking in the necessary intelligence a clever dispatch rider.

The sad experiences which the Russians had with their Cossack troops should cause us to pay increased attention to the selection of our cavalry recruits.

As long as the often expressed wish of the cavalry to have a representative on the " Assenting Commissions " is not carried out, the cavalry will not receive those recruits which are most suitable.

With reference to a war this is much to be deplored.

" The use of cavalry dismounted is only exceptional "—with these words is introduced the section about dismounted service in our regulations (Part II.).

Agreed! We have already given our reasons in another place why, in spite of the experiences of the Russo-Japanese War, we hold fast to the view that the sword is the principal weapon— the *ultima ratio*—of cavalry.

In spite of a true persistence in the principle laid down, it would never occur to-day to any thinking cavalryman to dispute " that the exceptional use of cavalry dismounted " of which the regulation speaks will be in a future war, so to say, our daily bread.

A good cavalry ought to have decidedly learnt in peace-time to feel themselves at home in the firing-line.

The command " With rifles, dismount !" must not mean anything out of the common.

The Austro-Hungarian cavalry practises the fight dismounted with that traditional conscientiousness which it brings into every detail of the service.

When one takes into consideration the time and trouble expended, it appears to us that the results obtained still leave much to be desired.

Many of our detachments, so active on horseback, betray, as soon as the carbine is in their hands, a certain clumsiness and helplessness.

This is to be observed both during field practices as well as on manœuvres.

The cause is due to the fact that the instructors—*i.e.*, in the first place, the officers—for the most part are wanting in the necessary infantry routine.

As the idea of the thing is more or less strange to them, they generally cling much too anxiously to the forms laid down in the drill-books.

Where are our young officers to obtain a familiarity with the rules and appearances of the modern infantry fight ?

At any rate, the students of the Neustadt Academy, who practise for two years under suitable instruction the practical duty of infantry, could acquire an idea of it. The candidates for cavalry at that Academy, however, as a rule, think it below their dignity to expend the necessary interest on these matters.

In most cases they do not carry away with them to their regiments an appreciable understanding of musketry.

It is still more unfavourable in this respect with the cavalry cadets and the one-year volunteers who are appointed regular officers.

They can learn only the formal part of the infantry training from their *pro tem.* instructors, as the latter do not know much more themselves.

The " further courses " at the Army Musketry School, to which every year a few older cavalry officers are sent, have more the purpose of increasing their technical knowledge than the practical side of their training. This does not help much to train the men in fire action.

Our opinion is that the best means of getting rid entirely of this evil would be to attach a sufficient number of officers and non-commissioned officers of the infantry as instructors to cavalry regiments. The officers and non-com-

missioned officers would only require to be
taken away from their own arm during the
afternoon, so far as it is a question of the same
garrisons.

The proposed means must obtain during two
different periods: Firstly, during the individual
instruction of the recruit; secondly, at the time
of squadron training. For the present it would
be advisable that the musketry field practices
should take place everywhere under the direction
of infantry officers. Devotion to duty and the
zeal of our cavalry officers answer for it that in
a few years, following the plan described, they will
have acquired the necessary routine which is now
failing them, and will be able to dispense entirely
with the help of the infantry.

Of course our regulation, which always must
form the first rule as far as the fight dismounted
is concerned, must undergo a revision according to the modern idea. For many of the ideas
laid down are absolutely discredited by the
experiences of the Russo-Japanese War — for
example, the volley, to which such a decisive
importance is ascribed, and, during the attack,
the advance of the whole squadron at the same
time, etc.

The lessons of the late campaign have shown
that in the future only a strong cavalry, equipped
with all the appliances of modern science, will be
able to carry out their allotted duty.

In theory, therefore, the demand for a considerable addition to the strength of our cavalry is justified.

Its strength in proportion to the other arms is at a greater disadvantage than in any other of the armies of the Great Powers.

However, on account of the financial and political condition of our monarchy, all reform in this respect, unfortunately, is as good as impossible.

Instead of advancing useless proposals, let us try something more practical, and see whether at least other means cannot be taken which may strengthen our cavalry equally well.

Above all, let us ask for a suitable war organization for this arm.

The divisional cavalry played less than a modest part in the Russo-Japanese War. There is no deed of arms by the divisional cavalry worth recording either on the side of the Russians or the Japanese.

At the most we see them prolonging the infantry firing-line with the few rifles at their disposal at different times—as, for example, in the fight at Wafankou, the 3rd Japanese cavalry regiments on the right wing of the 3rd Division.

The cavalry attached to the Japanese infantry at the battle of Liaoyang were put to a peculiar use. It had to cook the food for the infantry fighting in front, and carry it into the firing-line—

perhaps a very practical use, but scarcely corresponding to the rules laid down for the employment of this arm. We will not reproach the divisional cavalry, forced into the entrenched line of battle which stretched for many miles, that during the battle they could not perform anything.

An opportunity for divisional cavalry to act, as is suggested in our regulations, will at best occur in the future if it is employed with an infantry division fighting on a flank.

On the other hand, it must appear strange that the divisional (army corps) cavalry, strong as they were on both sides, could not even perform their proper duty—*i.e.*, local reconnaissance—without the help of others. With the Russians, the mounted scout detachments of infantry regiments were used for choice.

With the Japanese, detachments composed of infantry and cavalry took over the duties of the necessary reconnaissance.

In the face of these facts, can we maintain that the apportionment of a whole cavalry regiment (of three squadrons) to each Japanese infantry division was not a great mistake on the part of the Commander-in-Chief ?   The small strength of the cavalry available (fifty-five squadrons) in no way justifies such a waste. By a more careful apportioning, which, certainly, would have produced no disadvantage that could be felt—for example, half a regiment to an infantry division—another complete independent cavalry division could have been formed.

That its existence at Mukden would have been everything in the scale there is no doubt.

On the side of the Russians we find no divisional cavalry in the real sense of the word.

On the other hand, cavalry was apportioned in varying strengths and organization to the army corps, according to what was wanted (or fancied !).

At Mukden, for example, the 1st Siberian Army Corps had available over 6 squadrons ; 17th European, over 12 ; 3rd Siberian, over 18.

This, again, is an unjustifiable weakening of the independent cavalry. On the other hand, the principle of apportioning cavalry entirely to the army corps, and not to the divisions, is certainly correct, so far as the great army masses are concerned.

The battle organization of our field army shows the same fault with which we have just reproached the Japanese.

We as well, with our relatively weak cavalry force, have no reason to distribute it excessively. Three squadrons for each infantry division means a superfluous luxury which we decidedly cannot allow ourselves, because, for the three or four field armies which we place in the field in the event of war, the five or six independent cavalry divisions are too few.

We have altogether fourteen army corps—we

cannot include the 15th (Bosnian) for special reasons—to provide with the necessary cavalry.

One of our six squadron regiments placed at the disposal of the corps commanders would be quite enough for this purpose.

This gives, on an average, 2 squadrons for every one of the 42 regular and Landwehr infantry divisions ; therefore a saving of 42 squadrons from the organization at present in force.

Remaining still to form the independent cavalry divisions would be 264 squadrons (including the imperial and royal Landwehr and Honved formations).

From these could be formed 11 divisions of 24 squadrons, sufficient to give to each army a cavalry corps of from 2 to 3 cavalry divisions. Sooner or later it will have to be decided— analogous to the Germans and French—to form our army corps out of only two infantry divisions.

Hand in hand with this regulation must then take place the change in the organization of our cavalry which is so much to be wished for—*i.e.*, 4 squadron regiments. Eighty-seven of such would be formed in this manner, of which 21 would be army corps cavalry, and the remaining 66 would be able to be formed into independent cavalry divisions.

Then it would be a matter of opinion whether one should make them 6 or 4 regiments strong. As logically more correct, we prefer the latter.

Then, by these means, we should obtain the imposing number of 16½ divisions.

Then the force of cavalry would really become an independent unit for all cavalry enterprises. By the continual growth of modern armies the army corps has practically become the strategical unit in the place of the division.

From this follows the logical necessity of placing the reconnoitring machine at the disposal of the former instead of the latter.

Should one of its infantry divisions receive an independent mission—be it only as advance-guard, flank-guard, or something of the same sort—then the corps commander has with him the necessary cavalry to give. Under these circumstances he would give the whole cavalry regiment which was at his disposal.

According to our practice at manœuvres at the present time the divisional cavalry—with the exception of the legendary three information patrols—really forms a reservoir from which is provided a number of small detachments to the different infantry columns, mounted orderlies, and messengers for all the higher commanders.

What then remains after this mischievous splitting up is far too weak to give any sort of energy to local reconnaissance. Trotting ahead within proper distance of the infantry advance-guard, there is nothing left to the small force, when sighting the head of the hostile infantry, but to retire to one of the wings, and there in all modesty to wait to the end of the fight.

Here and there the slumbering desire for action is given vent to by some heroic deed, such as an attack on hostile artillery, which in actual war could never have taken place.

The army corps cavalry ought to be employed on quite different principles.

In order to carry on with a united force, and regardless of extraneous calls on them, their principal task, reconnaissance, they should be spared at other times.

Their extremely small volume of fire, in comparison with the infantry, would be better employed during the fight only in cases of necessity.

On the other hand, the final act of the fight should find them ready, side by side with the independent cavalry, to reap the result of a victory, or to hinder the hostile cavalry from converting the defeat of their own army into a rout.

However much we protest against the splitting up of the cavalry corps for minor duties, we at the same time recognize that the infantry divisions should not be left without cavalry for patrolling locally, for security on the march, and, finally, for providing messengers and orderlies.

However, they can, and must, manage this duty with two troops of " staff cavalry."

This could more easily be managed if bicycle

detachments were formed, like the Prussian Colonel Gaedke has repeatedly proposed.

Our ingenious organization of country horses and the abundance of cavalry reservists make it possible to organize an increased number of " staff troops," as well as to keep them at their full strength.   One will decidedly have to reckon with the wastage of a great number of these detachments.

It would be a good thing if the higher infantry commanders were accustomed in peace manœuvres to treat more economically and carefully the cavalry which they are given.   Now the divisional cavalry is often treated in a manner which, in real war, would certainly cause its complete disappearance in the course of a few days.

If our independent cavalry is to play in future wars the important active and independent rôle for which we hold it to be absolutely predestined, then the peace organization has still to take steps for this ideal :

1. That the cavalry divisions, which it is intended to form, shall be organized in exactly the same manner in which they will enter the field.

2. That the horse artillery shall be correspondingly increased.

3. That a machine-gun detachment of four pieces shall be formed for each division.

To the first is still to be added : It appears to be especially necessary to avoid as far as possible, in the event of mobilization, the formation of new regiments or organizations by the cavalry arm.

In war it is a matter of daily occurrence for every cavalry leader to have to trust subordinate detachments with independent duties of the most different kinds.

It is therefore of the greatest importance that he should know his subordinates thoroughly well in peace—not only what their service capabilities are, but also as regards their character.

As this requirement was not met when transferring guard and line cavalry officers *en masse* to the Cossack regiments of the Manchurian Field Army, the measure did not meet with the success which the staff of the Russian army had expected.

To the second : As Austria-Hungary, according to its organization, only possesses 8 horse battery divisions, each of 12 guns, therefore by the creation of 11 (or 16) cavalry divisions 6 (or 16) new horse batteries require still to be formed.

Twelve guns are the least with which a horse division can do.

To the third : Not a moment should be lost in the creation of the necessary machine-gun detachments (11 to 16).

The opinion of experts, who had an opportunity of observing quite close the working of this new weapon, is that machine-guns are most suitable for increasing the volume of fire of troops—but only in the case where the latter have a thorough knowledge of their tactical use.

Correctly posting them at the commencement of a fight is one of the chief arts of using them ; for to undertake a change of position is, in most cases, a difficult manœuvre. Above all, the location of the machine-guns too early by the enemy is a great drawback.

As the number of gunners serving them must always be fairly limited, it is of the greatest importance that the cavalry on emergency should be in a position to replace them.

Everything demands that, in peace-time, cavalry every year should be thoroughly exercised in the use of machine-guns. Till now, unfortunately, only a few of our regiments have had this opportunity during the Kaiser manœuvres.

It is self-evident that cavalry leaders should have the opportunity during the manœuvres of practising the tactics of the battle raids which we have sketched. The relatively short time the fights at the manœuvres last, however, forms a great obstacle in this respect ; for the slow development of the modern battle, lasting for days, is an essential preliminary to the carrying out of our tactical proposals.

At peace manœuvres one has to be content, in most cases, with only indicating the extensive movements which have been planned. At all events, one will have to finally discard the passive manner of guarding the flanks. That we are on the high road to it is shown by the fervid activity of the cavalry divisions which took part the other day in the Silesian Kaiser manœuvres.

If the spirit of initiative is really present, it is certain to fix itself in the right grooves in war.

We, as well as our German allies, shall have to disaccustom ourselves to attacks in masses against victorious advancing infantry "to relieve the pressure on our own infantry."

They are undertaken at manœuvres mostly for show only.

The well-known, and, as regards the cavalry arm, exceptionally clear-thinking Prussian military writer, Colonel Gaedke, justly remonstrates against this practice, which might eventually find in war such a fatal imitation.

Nothing is further from us than to propose to the cavalry that they should take anxious care to prevent great losses. The difficulties of filling up their ranks again give them, on the other hand, not only the right, but the duty, to see by all their operations whether the loss and the results obtained are commensurate with one another. In this respect, however, in the last war, the balance is decidedly too much in favour of their own preservation. The extremely small losses of both cavalries in the Russo-Japanese War in comparison with the other arms makes a cavalry officer somewhat ashamed. A cavalry which is thoroughly conscious of its duty will, in every war, be in that position where it must stick at nothing, even if it should suffer the greatest losses.

This will, above all, happen where it is a question of obtaining at any price a knowledge of the hostile manœuvre zone.

As seeing is often not possible without going quite close to the enemy, it appears to be of the greatest importance to avoid carefully anything which might lead to an early discovery. This recognition ought to decidedly cause a thorough reform in the clothing and equipment of the cavalry. Especially we Austrians ought not to hide from ourselves the fact that the uniform of our cavalry is conspicuous, can be seen from a long distance, and therefore is very unpractical.

The red riding breeches, the bright braided slung jacket, the light blue ulankas and tunics (the latter frequently covered with glaringly coloured facings), the glittering Dragoon helmets, the sparkling sword scabbard and buckles, the gold cross-belts of the officers—this is not at all suitable for war.

At the commencement of the campaign the Japanese also were wearing red riding breeches and tunics braided in a similar manner.

Within a short time, however, they were obliged to hide the red colour with a covering of khaki colour. We Austrians cannot take our stand upon

6

tradition as an excuse for retaining the bright cavalry uniforms as, for example, the Germans do with a certain amount of right. For our authorities had already, after 1866, broken with all tradition when they altered the time-honoured, historical white tunic of the infantry, which, as is well known, was not taken into the field, and changed the really tasteful dress of the Lancers, Hussars, and Cuirassiers. The introduction of a khaki-coloured or grey field uniform, with quite inconspicuous rank and regimental badges, should be adopted without delay. All which makes an officer conspicuous at a distance should be done away with.

A patrol which comes into range of the enemy's fire should not stand the chance of losing their leader first of all.

In the place of the heavy Dragoon helmet, Lancer caps, and Hussar busbies, which are beyond measure so unpractical, and which would in a very short time lose all their ornaments, they could wear a lighter felt hat.

All shining buttons, buckles, and other such-like parts should share the fate of the helmet.

The heavy riding-boots, which after a few marches and bivouacs are scarcely to be got on, should be replaced by ankle-boots and gaiters of some waterproof material.

Further, strap spurs should replace box spurs. A cloak to hook on made out of coarse cloth, and for the winter a fur coat reaching to the knees, felt overshoes, fur gloves, and on the head-dress a covering which should have a protector for the ears, should complete the equipment. Now we must hasten to allay the secret fears of young officers over the unornamental uniform which we have described. Perhaps we shall succeed in doing so by declaring that we are all for retaining a suitable and effective peace uniform, in addition to a suitable campaign dress, which is only to meet practical requirements.

In military questions we must give quite a serious amount of thought to psychological facts.

We must also take into consideration human weaknesses. The Austro-Hungarian cavalry officer especially must not be grudged the little halo that still surrounds the arm he has chosen, if we consider how much he is suffering from bad garrisons, hard service, and material frugality.

An elegant and effective uniform consoles young men in many privations and gives them self-respect, a quality which decidedly promotes the desire to distinguish one's self in battle. The ordinary cavalryman also, who in peace has to perform a more fatiguing service, accompanied with greater bodily risk, than his comrade in the infantry, deserves a uniform in which he can "cut a dash." Let us retain as parade and walking-out dress the one we have now, or, better still, that which was in vogue before 1866.

6—2

But for all other occasions let us introduce as soon as possible the campaign uniform sketched above.

Although all the other arms have made a trial of such a uniform, it is to be regretted that the cavalry are still an exception.

In Germany it appears that they are also guilty of the same neglect. Whoever, at the manœuvres there, has seen each cavalry detachment betrayed too early by the white straps, the light tunics and slung jackets, and the glittering weapons, can only wish such fine-looking regiments were not compelled to appear thus clad before the enemy.

If it is really wished to limit as much as possible the visibility of our cavalry, the disappearance of grey horses from the ranks is a measure that can no longer be avoided.

Whoever has led a reconnoitring patrol will certainly remember with pleasure cases where, at a great distance, on a mountain slope or top, a grey horse suddenly appearing has put him on the right scent, and in this way been the initial cause of an excellent report.

We would sooner not make it so easy for the enemy. Austria-Hungary is rich enough in horses to be able to refuse greys as cavalry remounts.

The Japanese cavalry, in spite of small numbers and bad material, thanks to the splendid spirit which inspired them, did their duty to the best of their ability.

This fact conceals an important lesson for us, who look upon the undeniable tactical and technical advantages of our cavalry with a certain amount of self-satisfaction : let us not prize too low, in the face of the splendid achievements attained in peace-time, the worth of the moral qualities, and never let us neglect fostering them.

In the greater part of our men exists still at bottom a healthiness neither weakened by the spirit of the times nor by national dispute. From this kernel of healthiness we can discern, perhaps not all, but surely a great proportion of, the splendid soldierly virtues with which their religion and ethics imbue the Japanese. Our officers must always be equal to this high task. A high-mindedness, self-sacrificing devotion to duty, and love of the profession must never be lost. This demand is easy to assert but—do not let anyone be deceived—difficult of fulfilment.

The position and material existence of the officer is to-day scarcely such as to make him especially the upholder of a departing ideal.

Our higher officers, who, as regards this point, spring from a more favourable period, should always remember this. They should consider it one of their chief duties to lighten the struggle for existence of their younger comrades as far as the interests of the service will allow.

A slavish submission of junior officers should

never be permitted, but a willing obedience should always be required which does not restrain the development of their own individuality.

Who has not the courage of his own opinions in peace-time, in war will certainly not be brought to that sense of responsibility which should be the attribute of every cavalry officer. The worry of insignificant work, from which our subalterns and indeed squadron leaders, on account of pressure "from above," frequently and without necessity suffer, uses up too early their best powers, limits their horizon, and makes them ill-humoured and incapable of independent enterprises.

Only officers trained in aristocratic and sympathetic principles will make the right sort of instructors for our men.

The old military truth, "What is not inspected will not be practised," in a certain sense applies equally well in the psychological province.

The spirit which animates a unit should have more weight in the judgment of a commander than purely military performances.

It is certainly not easy in peace-time to get a clue for ascertaining the moral worth of a body of troops.

A superior who is a little psychological, and has his heart in the right place, will, by a number of small signs, even in this respect be able to come to a right conclusion.

In the first place, regimental commanders ought to start the moral education of their men on the right lines.

A colonel who is lacking in high-mindedness and sympathy, in our opinion, is unsuited to his position, even should he be a cavalry officer of the first rank.

Unfortunately, with us it sometimes appears as if our authorities were not quite of that mind.

Field officers, who have really nothing more in their favour except that they are so-called " good soldiers " and have the whole of the regulations at their fingers' ends, are very often given the all-important charge of a regiment.

A not quite unobjectionable interpretation of the conception " good soldier " has been adopted by us during the course of the long peace. He is found embodied in a personality which accommodates itself to circumstances, never worries its superiors, and which guesses the intentions of each superior officer, and, with true fanaticism, proceeds to carry them out.

If such a " good soldier " becomes a colonel, he naturally demands from those under him the same blind obedience which he himself has always practised.

To gain laurels at inspections is his highest dream. The inner consciousness of having done his duty to the best of his ability does not satisfy him.

In order to obtain the longed-for recognition from above, he becomes distracted, wishes to do everything himself, and drives his subordinates to desperation.

Soon these latter do their duty no longer with pleasure and love of their profession, but indifferently and mechanically. The spirit of the officers deteriorates and the better elements retire.

This in no way disturbs the strict colonel. So long as the duty is performed from morning to night, according to regulation, he does not care about the spirit. A firm rule of conduct for his manner of thinking and acting is entirely lacking.

For him the question is always, "What will the general or inspecting officer say to it?"

If in the above we have painted, in somewhat drastic colours in order to emphasize it, an evil which is without doubt present, there is a fact which cannot be denied—namely, that many good men, who are eminently suited as cavalry leaders, retire as captains.

The ideal which they sought in their profession is not fulfilled. Sooner than have their individuality forced from them in this way they prefer to retire.

Our friend the "red-tape" colonel will pass it over with the much-beloved platitude that nobody is irreplaceable.

We in no way agree with him.

Leaders in the Russian cavalry were decidedly

wanting who were known to possess intelligence, tactical knowledge, and desire for action, combined with the moral courage for responsibility, without which the former attributes are useless.

Whether we ought not more energetically to put a stop to the vicious aspiring and cringing in our ranks, so as to obtain a better record in this respect when, at some future time, it shall be our turn, may be left unanswered.

The leaders of great infantry masses will, in wars of the future, as far as physical comfort is concerned, have quite a bearable time. Even the fatigues of the day of battle will, as a rule, not be particularly severe on them.

For more than ever, in order to prevent a disturbance in the widespreading and complicated service of information and reports, are they bound to a fixed place far behind the fighting-line.

It is otherwise with the cavalry general. He cannot take with him luxurious carriages and collapsible houses made of wood or asbestos. For him it means sharing all physical exertions equally with the youngest soldier, and then being capable afterwards of brainwork.

It is therefore a necessity, even if a cruel rule, that the older cavalry captains, who have used up their physical activity during a long and worrying service as squadron commanders, should have to retire at the rank of major.

Another question is, whether we ought to imperil

physically our most qualified experts by wearing them out in the rank of captain owing to a too slow promotion.

We answer it with a decided "No."

The last campaign, again, proved that the conditions of modern war make it almost harder to produce a Seydlitz, Murat, or Stuart, than a Moltke.

Herein lies the warning for cavalry officers to cherish and promote with unceasing care those physical and moral qualities which make up a cavalry leader.

If this succeeds, then we need not fear for the future; for the machine is good.

THE END

BILLING AND SONS, LTD., PRINTERS, GUILDFORD

KORTSIN

Kang ping sien

SHEN

KIN CHOFU

Chau yang

I chou

Kwang ning

Sin min

Liao Ho

Niuchwang

Hai chöng

An shun cha

Tien chwang tai

Port Niuchwang
(Ying kou)
(TREATY FORT)

Liao Ho

Ying yuen

Kai ping

GULF OF LIAO TUNG

Siung yue chong
Saddle I.

Fu chou

Society Bay

Ching hang I.

Hulu chan B.

Nan kwan

Kwang-tung Peninsula

Kin chau

Dalny

Ta lien Bay

RUSSIAN TERRITORY

PORT ARTHUR

Liau ti chan Promontory

Ta la shan I.

Elliot Is.

Blonde I.

KORE

North Latitude

Scale of
20   10   0   20

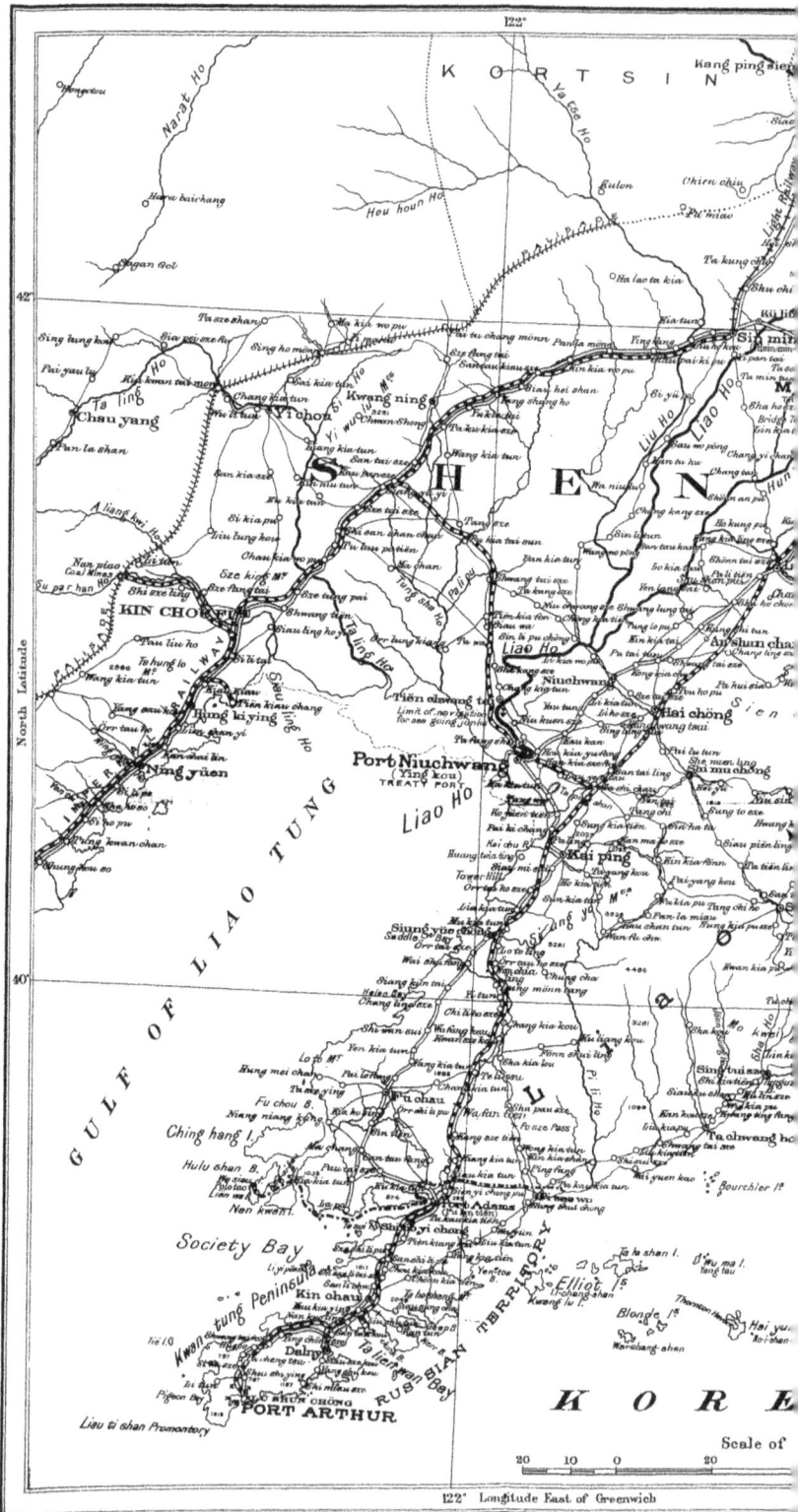

122° Longitude East of Greenwich

London: H

KDEN
Tieling hsien
Chang tu fu
Kai Yuan

Mukden

Sin min pu
Tung hua sien
PING TING SHAN
KANG   KING
SHAN LING

Wu nu shan
Huai yen sien
Yalu R.

Fong wang chöng

To shui hua

Chen seng
Ku ben chung
Antung
Wiju
Ta ku shan

Yalu Riv.
(Am. nok gan)

Chak to

Chon chu
Seng chong
An chu
(An-ju)

Pyöng yang

Chinampo

A   B   A   Y

Ping Yang Inlet

English Miles
40   60   80   100

Stanford's Geog.l Estab.t London

www.ingramcontent.com/pod-product-compliance
Lightning Source LLC
Chambersburg PA
CBHW031001090426
42737CB00008B/622